AFTER-IMAGE

DENNIS SCOTT

PEEPAL TREE

First published in Great Britain in 2008
Peepal Tree Press Ltd
17 King's Avenue
Leeds LS6 1QS
UK

ISBN 13: 9781845230241

ARTS COUNCIL ENGLAND Peepal Tree gratefully acknowledges Arts Council support

CONTENTS

AFTER-IMAGE

When this machine is dead
the poems it made will flare
wild, flower, will echo the slipped cog
rusting like blood. The petals will engage
as accurately as teeth, cutting
the line short.
Stems will continue to hurl the head's career
in some automatic transmission of dream:

the tired metal stammers, breaks, is bled.
Its images persist;
repeating softly
what the metal said.

TRACK: HEALSONG

In the locked dark
before music

when you have heard the one
very clear tone
that means the skin has come open
the light has made a slit wide enough

reach in. Break that cold flower
where it cancers
sharp into the eye. The nerves will snap
tight as guitars
the drum will stitch your face together, slowly
as roots
the horn's cry will tongue your cut
clean.
Scream.

See.

LAST POEM

Wanted to give
you something finally to echo,
crystal, unflawed.
Remembered in time
you must heat sand from the hour-glass
in your own tight mouth, till pressure
fuses the easy word
to soft, white silence.
Mould it in the skull's round
make it all
yours.
When it cools, clear shell of your life,
break it.
Listen.

NEGATIVE

From the chalk hills, land
runs out its tongue
South-West, savouring the sea;
lolls a windy noon.
The aeroplanes like flies
come in, are undisturbed,
and leave. They have
seen all this
before. At one

precisely, it rains,
and the filming pink
of your summer dress
darkens. We gather them,
shoes, key, radio, biscuits, towel –

image:
        shutter quick, my memory
is as sharp as cactus,
the hurt of it,
snags at your dress
and you turn as

then, help me, it's caught
and sensibly
I should have
frozen you there
forever, camera shy, laughing
to tell you, to tell you
but the rain blurred
my care and the summer's
unprinted

today. A pink dress
furled some woman down
to the runway
and I would have forgotten
we made no promises

when it rained
precisely

BALLADE

For those who give their hearts away
like a frequent miracle, whose breath
flickers between the storms of love
like a travelling candle
any may set burning,
here is scarred driftwood
and a wind to float moonshine by
and a tune to sing to sleep:

A boy spat out a seed once
and it grew
the height of his beanstalk dreams
till they made
a ship to rove in from it, tarred and timbered,
a rich sea farer
for untold ventures, to sail
under shifting storms, sea
shanties lifting
the cabin-boy's shadow by lamplight taller
than thunder, than
the shining needle of the wet ship's mast
dancing, or the moon.

Now all the sailors are sleeping
and their children
forgotten too, and the boy
has eaten his fill
of world's wonder, and hungers
no more, and the timber has drifted down
and down to a distant shore –
see, it lies there, near
two lovers who woke this evening
to the moon, and scratched their names
by its light

for ever and ever –
not hearing the sand sing

of change. I warn all
those who must weather the world,
all we like ships who sail down time
in a paper-thin tenderness.

OPEN

Today, work
waiting, I make poems. But
the room's too small to turn
words in. On an impulse of rain
open the windows, hoping
this itch and dry of images will change.
I rearrange desk to the air,
shifting my chair.

– And suddenly the eye
examines wet leaves, pencilling
their fragile paper weight
on the lawn's green table, fluent lizards
writing their sentences of joy,
a green bud's stamp
posted on twigs, a mail-box red flower's
effortless fall
down.

It's a new house
I live from, suddenly guest,
I rest often not writing
between the wind's idle
idle, familiarizing trees
as worn as dictionaries,
learning still the phonemes
of a bird's trill.

Never knew
such world or such dimension
possible as poems woven
from simple things
changed in their weaving
myself. It's all there, all.
Next time I shan't wait
for the rain to fall.

ANOTHER COUNTRY

Willing an upright, not so
stubborn spine, he blotted
the water house with his mountain back.
There, fish ploughed that tideless kingdom,
spring ever below the flat sky
among snails' flow and fresh weeds.
He saw them, thirsty. Pebbles,
a white house of shell,
a plastic oyster clapped itself together
the fish performed and the pump
in the bi-valve; bubbles rose
more liquid than air,
silver and floating home.

He hunchbacked, less capable,
real and less still than the effortless country
that tided it fish-deep day long
stared; curl of his fingers
loose printed the glass, denying
that sharp of his eyes. Diamond stare
cut holes in the harbour of green tank
till he swam too, cut close
by the swift bellies, the painted tails.
His eyes were no larger than scales
floating down through the plain air, wet,
weighing the risks of element
foreign but kinder than that
he stood in.
Out of his shell humped
he slid, breathing easy, followed
his eyes' clear path to the comforting
exile, unselfing, among fish.
Waved the soft space with their thin
emerald and gold, languid; sleek

as they, he: unshaped to a fine
and balancing beauty, suspending his shadow
on pebbles and oyster, hearing
like welcome the drum of the bubbles
beating to paradise, part of a rounding
and high, unpredictable dance
through the water green
weeds among snails walking on glass
down and grey, gliding.

                                        Fish only
talked of his coming, his taking
the shell for his house and rocking
and sleep, accustomed by now
to unchanging, breath given away. Unused
to this living, he drowned.

And the fish were placid, performing,
since born to grace, breathing water
as fish can, the snails promenaded
that thin glass wall
past the smudge of his fingers
as snails will
the weed lay still, and the bubbles
rose more liquid than sleep than
blood tirelessly pumped,
and the oyster applauded. But the landlady
drummed at the door and screamed
till they took him away
floating sleek in his wet mind's centre;
still humped.

AT DIFFERENT SPEEDS

A woman rolls the cotta up
and lifts her load.
A cow swings by.
A tick-bird follows, hungry, cutting
a white line down the road.
The red light stares me to a stop.
They wander past – cow, woman, bird...

THIRD WORLD BLUES

I go among the fashionable drums
trying to keep true my own blood's subtle beat.
Something of darkness here, of jazz-horn heat,
but something too of minuet; it hums
cool in my voice, measures my heart, my feet
strictly. And not all the blues, the concrete
jungles of this Third World, mine, can defeat
that pale and civil music when it comes.

So I make my own new way; I entreat
no tribal blessing or honour. I build –
lonely a little – my house. It is filled
with ghosts, with their summoning air, I greet
them all; their tunes, their joys mine. I advance,
my feet bare to a strangely patterned dance.

A KIND OF KARATE

When I no longer pretended
we differed
(yet also the same
in my skull)
the days became very simple
and disturbing like metal knives.

They grew tall as my house.
I remember the garden
we played in as round
as a dream
my love, contracted
to that space
                    hedged
by his dangerous envy
I wanted forever
to be quiet with him, guiltless;
determining peace by my own kind
of friendship.

This morning I wake
and look,
someone has spread the rough map
of here out – mountains, the tiled
town quiet and home –
land under our heels,
shining like knives the sea a-
bout; dojo, mat of my country.

I call to him, what is
this terrible thing
you require, smiling
he whispers the ritual
challenge:

"I come to you
with my hands
empty."

JUMPSONG: FOR JIMMY TURNER AND THE NTD*

Look. Straight up. Takes off, turns,
riff and
tuck, nothing round him
the trampoline gusts
the earth swings under, hung from his feet,
he signs the air
with his whole person,
crystal. My stare flicks it, it rings
true. Here is what that sound sings:

Look! Straight up! I can,
my skin fits, it goes with me,
I know
now to tell the end of every nerve
now!
how to give
in,
to go through
the terrible places
where no one attends
to fall
up
like Ornette's low blue laughter
against the beat, holding the next
time higher,
to enter the silence
with my hands open
to mark your eye
like a gull cut on a crystal glass

I know my weight.

* National Theatre of the Deaf

THE MUSIC MAN

He's crying for some
where kind
blows a hurting trumpet
improvising
notes like a rainy afternoon
colours
my mind blue

through the window
like a half remembered road
going home
travelling blind.
How will I get there, music man?
What will I find?

DIRECTED BY ME: FOR JOY

What I don't like about home movies
is that sooner or later you stop
running to me through the grass,
not like those pictures where the long shot says
forever
and untouchably the maiden floats
between the wind. Soft
centre.
        With us, after a little you're that close
that I can smell the onions of your lunch,
and there's no way I can pretend I didn't
forget to wash the dishes, and your nose
shines, and your dress was new once.
On the other hand, the script is new.
I like surprises. And it's kind of nice
that you're running in my direction.
Especially when nobody except you can
ever edit me out.

CUBE SONG

All the dances of my life
are in your hand,
turn me, turn me
in your hand
I'll be just a step away,
change my patterns, I will be
all the dances that you see –

All the colours of my life
are in your hand,
turn me, turn me
in your hand
I will be a thing of light,
paint me rainbow, I will be
all the colours that you see –

All the lyrics of my life
are in your hand,
turn me, turn me
in your hand
I will be the perfect song,
play me softly, you will hear
music, music everywhere

UNDERGROUND

there is silence, you say.
The mongoose rests at the bamboo hill,
gnawing roots. The insects make holes
through the moth's tongue, it withers like bark.
We come and go.
The earth's curve is imperceptible.

But I am not deceived. I fall
as quickly as any sparrow
towards the fire,
past the dumb gone
round the corner of patience,
past the green survivors.
The roots hold me in
place. I have been there
before, to the river, I remember
where it leaps and is ever
underground, I know
the song of the knotted fire
where everything becomes simple
and must be spoken.
I am not deceived.

UNICORN

The singers die; their songs remain to show
how every beauty but the songs will go.

There is a Unicorn no more may tire
than I cut from my flesh Time's cancering weave;
and these alembic images I fire
to honour him are all that I shall leave
to mark his passings by my door:
clear, dainty hooves, his spoor.

Where are the worlds that promised joy or woe?
Gone where all beauties but his breath shall go.

I do not know his form. He, pale as air
assumes the shape of any changeless thing.
My Lady laughs – and suddenly He's there.
Or dimly, echoed in a high bird's wing,
there's follow fire; it is his thigh
gleams whitely as a sigh.

Where the rose bloomed, not even thorns now grow;
gone where all beauties but that horn must go.

By day, by night; lost in an old man's eyes
I've seen his traces. Love has bid him keep
her secret signs. The wicked and the wise
dream him; he eats the honey of their sleep.
Then with such lines I celebrate
that slow, delicate gait.

For where's the wind I thought would always blow?
Gone. Every beauty but this breath will go.

SEEDSONG

The bird
having come a long way
circles, hungry.
A flat land, a city of stones.
In the cemetery a few small things are growing.
The seed's edge takes the sun's falling fire like jewels.
It is too late to leave; the wind is rising
blowing the graves deeper.
The bird eats quietly, stropping its beak
against a stone with no name.
In the morning it moves on.
I see it passing my window, going surely
to some place I have never known.
It shits on my neat
green
garden.

I do not know
what will grow.

MATADOR

Your clock's tic
toc tic toc, the toreadors
withdraw, the horses of the night
are dragged away.
                    Brittly, we dance.
Words brush like sand under
the drift, slow pivotings of anger,
the hesitating turn.
                    My body moves
its casual evasion, cape
in an empty ring where you can't
hear the wind, the questions. They give up
a bitter whisper; sand
on my mouth.
                    Idly the hollow moon
burns with a circular fire. And
                    between
your eyes, in your eyes, I
have placed (what bright flowers
they put out!) faultlessly
as a picador, the pale spears of my silence.
I arrange my feet
in a strict and angular courtesy,
I approach over the ritual sand
of my sadness.   I approach. You

may think it is only the red moon's shape
perceived dimly in waiting, perhaps
you will not notice this sharp, paper
sword of my love, nor see, dazzled
by danger, how hard it is, this
kill for my heart.

BLOOM TENDER

She expects him. Her barren
house welcomes his brazen
and jubilant coming.
                    The neighbours peer,
for what does he take her? Believe this:
his hands are full
of metal flowers. Their jangle
blazes and blooms with echo
the copper of loneliness, petals
have edges as sharp as
the lip of bells, their bronze leaves
are sharp and cutting;
the crimson falls
drop by drop from his fingers
his bones, his bones
are white cracks widening through
dry copper stems.

                    Where are you going, lover,
                    bearing these knife-cool blooms
                    past the wide-eyed neighbours
                    gasping in their rooms?

His feet go simply, like servants
they make no sound, his bare feet
touch the stone of her pathway
each flower peals his gift
in the afternoon silence. Hurting
and head one side, he listens
to copper bells burning
that door open, tilting to flowers
that ring between steps, come
come,
                    but his slow shadow carries

a darker bouquet, less barbaric; antiphon
softer and dumb.
                    Where sweat roots,
where his feet go and the glisten
falls red from his knuckle,

green trees grow.

JOURNEY

I enter the wilderness of your love.
Through the branching lust
of your limb-silence, wet,
I journey

between their green tongues
slow among tangles
your hair
moss and fern-smell
and the long twisted orchids
of your voice

velvet
down the path, rustle,
any track, any choice smooth
as cool stone, sun
leaps to my skin
down high leaves, and a solitaire
swift as your hand's touch
pierces the wind one
note by one, the parakeet
of passion caws
air to fire, cries
once, cries

clearing.
Centre. A bird
sits, eating
the spiders of your doubt
your mouth
everywhere. I wait.

I have given my face
to the red sharp mouth of your want

it has eaten my eyes
out. Shall lie here.

And wilderness will grow
with ancient slowness into
the holes, the air
shall close over all wound,
grass thicken, bird
soar,
silence. Nothing to show
this time
and again, this
miraculous journey.

And though there are spiders
in each step birds
follow, hungry;
makes for a difficult leaving. Be kind.

I enter the wilderness of your love

blind.

THE SUNDAY LOVING

You my church, and this, bed-
rock of my faith.
Kneeling by you
no worship, but soul's ease
find, for you flower,
and I. I enter without haste, aware
to the steady bell like veins
in the Sunday skin
of our waking.
On my tongue
your warm mouth's wafer taste
and palms, palms
open on that altar, here
is the world made flesh.
All won.

Twined
in this simple violence
I reaffirm
some Adam-bright response to joy,
some long ago gentle.
Your immediate sun
gathering my sparrow heart higher
by the window light, dimly,
among the ceremonies of desire
and your bright voice,
bells call.

I celebrate no fall, no
descent from grace,
the achievement of no cross.
Here I regain what is in us of loss,
found in your face.

FARMING

He makes her a poem
(she forks
wild flowers out of the grey afternoon)
she buries it, torn, like small white markers
into the skin of her silence.
She says, I am stone all the way
under. He smiles.

CONVERSATION

I send them out, trusting
myself as to any other journey.

Up wing. One, wheeling, kites high, winding.
But the closed sky turns it down: fails,
falls away from that calm
bowl like the socket of an eye, finds my mouth
a place to hide in, drowns
faultlessly.
The stiff air skews another. Hurls it again in
a single motion round the horizon of our laughter.
It comes back to my face with small cuts
smelling of cold, unable
to say what has happened. I nurse it quietly.
And one goes through, and through,
breaking the fat under the skin. Keeps on, not looking
back. Goes
on a pale track, beyond summons, beyond
reckoning. Lost
in his head like smoke.

Straggle them home: I learn that. For wrong questions
the penalty is silence, silence.

MINOS

I am trying
not to look at you
but your bright face
waits in the centre, still

that bull's eye
draws me delicately to
the centre of the labyrinth

where the king sits with kind hands
quiet, listens to my feet finding a way
to come without hurt
into the room

where he hides
where he waits
where he trusts

THE SUNDAY CORONATION

"...and I find that my stuff is getting so plain I am scared. You know, it simply becomes like a vase or a glass of water, or something..."

Derek Walcott

Queen in the house of my shadow,
ruler over areas bounded by my hands
outstretched, measures me drink. The tap glows
brass and tender, my child sleeps. Toast. Room
chair-straight and cool; no place
here, no time. Sunday reconciles
the bruised week, all the bare
bright skirmishes in the flag of your scarf,
and the kitchen clock tick –
because of your apron's fold
because of your feet without shoes –
muffles all morning, contains
this unofficial kingdom steady, slow.

My clinked knife breaks me wedges of content,
crumbs roll as bright as a silence
you shape round me, gold crumbs. No one
brings me water that leaps as slow
round in the wet glass, gathers light
from all corners of the young and yellow
Sunday like you, sovereign, sweet like water.

Now quiet wheels high, sipping peace
from the still air in my house, your
man served kindly; comfort now
over me, you bring simply
water, tasting of always.

Morning paper comes.
I wrap my calm in its crinkled news-smell
(water turning clears room clean) I attend
the court of your solstice. Queen of my heart
there are jewels of clear, wet loving
on your fingers, the sun
in the lensed glass circles us, joining.

Lingers

PARADOX

I dreamed you
fish, cutting the heavy sea
as soft as air,
trolling the coral silence of your pain
with silver care;

dreamed you whole
in the ground, rooted in dark,
imagined you tall like cane.
How strange the way
things leap
at once up to the hurling sun, down
into sleep –

twisting from shadow
falling away from light
we dance our life
in grief's eccentric wheel
somewhere
between flying to

and flight

TRACKSONG

Riding the trains without you
I fall out from home
into the dark, resisting
love's gravity
                                        the track's parabola
swings me away
along the evening's edge
                                                            I sit with strangers
listening: so many tales
in every silent face!
                                                        I watch
the stations touch and go. No
doubts, no dangers, no
decisions. In a little while
there will be promises to keep, but now
journey is its own end,
                                                            the towns
dream past my window, gone
before some person waking in that quiet house
can speak my name, or hear me go, or ask
when I'll be home.
                                                            The wheels are singing
between the shining cities.

CROSS COUNTRY

Driving, without you. Seemed a long way.
Would have turned back if I could have

found a place to, when
a girl with moths in her hair
thumbed me down.
I said, where from?
Her, she said, and there's a message.

But I forget now what it was.

> Something soft broke on the windshield
> flying
> blind to my light.
> I shivered, thinking –
> if it were you!
>
> Was.

Sometimes an ambulance
whines through the red
STOP

in my brain. Then like dust on the windshield, the
question:

will it reach us
in time?

STATEMENT

Once I would say
in the giving dances
in the youngtree shadows
what are you thinking
wanted to eat up your life
like naseberry flesh
roughsmoothcool

I was young then
blundered into love
wanting everything
in the hot evening
in the brown-ripe silences.

Now we are quiet together
at rest easily
tired
I watch your hand on my
skin
wrinkled over the hard seed
the tearshape secrets

I don't ask any more

BIRTHDAYSONG

What partners whispered come
what pleasures did you hear
and turn from, promenading
with me instead, year after year?
Would they have scored your face
as deep as children and my hands,
would they have measured it
to patience as we do?
I've watched you restless, hum
the waltzes from some other room, keyed
softer than my penny-whistle song.
Would they have beaten time? For all
the dances my love has denied you,
forgive; safe in the band that joins us
watch me jump – the carnival is passing.
I fret what tunes I can, dying beside you.

OBJECT LESSON

(Small boxes nose at the sidewalk
like boats,
a cheap doll tumbles down the culvert,
screaming.)

Once he dived
and came up, too
far from the ship.
Now the gutters are full of fin
subtle and sharp
in the broken mirror of his mind.
He falls headlong to
cracks in every street.
The shark haunts him.

Fish should be kept in bottles,
stared at,
and fed regularly.

MANUSCRIPT

That year
arranged you
on a clean page of my life
like a new poem. I read you, line by line
I learned your rhythms, calm and sure,
observing how your warm hand rhymed with mine.
No one had written on me so before.
I treasure that strange poem more and more.

ABSENCES

When the words have been
eaten through like dry lathes
and the house crumbles about
there are these

                    letters to you, hiding
among the chitinous shadows.
I read them stammering
as though by candlelight
a left, uncertain document
of some safe place

the insect wings of when
like leaves of wax, the poems

stiff and delicate
as japanese paper
in the wind and the rain,

in the wind and the rain,

where are the shelters of love
where is the roof of
your fingers
blessing my head?

WIFESONG

You are the road that leads to rest
You are the home that opens wide
You are the room curtained with peace
You are the silence at my side.
    Tie me closer, come what may,
    Tie me closer in your secret way.

You are the quiet ways I walk
You are the house I cannot leave
You are the room where my sleep waits
You are the thread my dreamings weave.
    Wind me closer, let me stay
    Wind me closer in your silken way.

DAY SIX

At first, hardly anything.   Footprints
sketched. Leafskin.
The seesaw is silent
as yet; the head, the heart weightless.
Furrows open out under the wind
that suggests breathing.
These will be muscle.

As the earth dries, the light falls more quickly.
It has blasted a rough shape out of the sand.
Stones for eyes.
Its tongue hangs rag-red from a thirsty shadow.
It doesn't move though. Not yet.

And the sun does not
grow less, it glints, it hammers down
on the air's mould.

The grains are fusing and becoming clear.
The nerves claw, and hook to.
Volition. Breath. Like a small scream.
Name it: Adam.

A SOUND OF BIRDS

Cockcrow. Morning. Wild birds. A sleeping sea.
Dark sand, and fisher nets on
twisted sticks. A solitary tree.
Long years ago a boy learns from his father
the waiting shape and grain of wood,
and makes, idly,
a crucifix.

Stones of love tremble at
the soldiers' feet –
                                        cockcrow.
                                                        Tears
in the torchlight – why is Peter crying?
The fire moves. Sword shimmers.
Sacrifice is near,
here. The crowd flickers. Moon
in a bowl of water
splinters in thirty.
Ecstasy begins.

Now leave the drunken smell
of fresh wood shavings and over
Galilee the April moon. Soon,
silence. Someone spits
in the dark sand of the courtyard.
Where are the birds, and why is Peter
crying?
                    Cockcrow!

Love is the subtlest treachery we know.

HELEN

Constantly, turns to the glass
oval, her face worn
dim as an artefact.
Do you remember, she says, smiling
(close the window, my love;
these evenings hurt my bones)
her smile writes thinly on the bone-
white room, graffiti cut in
the burnt walls of some ancient city.

No one will steal her again
(the town is fallen
away from her face) but proudly
she displays it, precious
as her carved stool, pottery,
the dried flower vase, her voice
becoming crystal and breaking –
turning from time to time
to glass, and back. It reflects
my thought – now no one writes me poems
she says, smiling. The corners of
her chair painted dark
by the dusted six o'clock
melancholy, talking, her face
as virgin as a temple whore's
(nights in that wide bed
pretending, she brushes her hair
and whimpers in her sleep
at the moon).

I scrawl this poem for her,
for the stone leaves of her
walling pride. When the flesh tallows
from her eyes' wick, and the very lip

is eaten away by the fire
of the falling sun
they will remember her
haunting her lust,
not believing that all
the battles are done,
and the glory
gone from her face;
till the last war is won
find her here, still, for
ever turning to her glass
in this white place

GUESTS

You walk through my blood
like small lights in a hundred rooms, you smile
and there are mirrors, you walk softly between
my hates and your hand caresses
some sleep-eyed beast,
perhaps your fingers are twined
in the white mane of a unicorn,
perhaps the whisper of hooves
like a shadow of laughing, perhaps
the glimmer of silence and white
like an echo of candles
your going like guests
through the rooms of my heart
on soft naked feet, your warm side
against his.
                    Poor beast
how he trembles
under your hands.

CUB

Here's an animal
home-skinned, two headed
and with his eyes shut
sleeping. He dreams
a little maybe, preferring
to hunt alone when
the real hunger doubles him
over in grief back
to positions of the one true
longing we share –
foetus.

          And game he plays!
(Easier as tournament goes
on) shapes his mood
to our eyes' reflection –
he's what now we wish
him to think he's made
of, boy.
          No kills yet
to his credit, not
weaned from kindness.

Till one noon
shrugging our love
for a bold new coat
he'll open his eyes
and his mouth wide as
the Guernica horse
to scream his coming –
of age at the trembling house
the walls will fall down
and the pack
take him to council as

one, they
recognizing some new beast
that walks the world without
mercy.

          But this one's special
(I've heard that each forked
creature goes singularly
and unduplicated,
he with two heads not least)

...one mouth roaring
the terrible hunger of his mind,
the other still, infinitely kind.

BAROMETER FALLING

In these latitudes
one may expect storm
without warning
air clears after
                    nothing
singular, a harmless passing
area of pressure
                    the geography of friendship
allows that trade
wind shift and nothing
really changes
the day's long spiral
on her couch
starswing
the quiet evenings of her contract
weather comes and goes
the land lies
no less constant, stronger
than passing turbulences, more enduring
than any sun king's rain.

A PERSONAL DOMESTICATION

Their welcome accommodates
his unexpected shape. The carpet
wrinkling to the colour of his mood, the air
swirls to a printed, cotton silence. Gently
they place the rods of their eyes along his
gestures, quick smiles cross
as slim as metal, make the cage
of his walking. He accepts
their approval; something, he sees,

is offered. In the cool, smooth dishes
of their attention, that hollow
his lightest words to an echo of truth,
they feed him their cautious love, their restless
fingers cracking the nuts of his unease,
and the hands that do not touch him
tender a sweet meat
amusement. Because he is hungry,
eats it, and pads out.

Then
the room shivers at last, and re-assumes
its warm and serviceable roughness,
the window closing like a sigh, the air
moves carelessly again, stilling.

But their dreams and their voices
taste of his acrid danger, attesting
something wild and shaggy came by
and walked on delicate claws
for fear of killing.

PRIVATE EYE

I have followed him
home in his room
ignoring the danger
he closes the door.
He removes his shoes and his
face, each layer of cloth
that makes his identity.
Soon, he's a stranger,
he polishes my eyes and poses
poring at me. Faithfully,
I reflect.
He moves dream heavy
now strips his skin
from over the muscles,
the fat, where it creases, peels
it like lampshade fabric
a welter of roses down
from his shanks. He's funny,
I can't help smiling
like a red, raw clown.
He opens the door,
hands me my hat.
When I am gone I hear him
screaming carefully all the time
I'm walking.
There's no explaining to you
the pleasure of stalking.

SERPENTSONGS

Prowl
This is how to go,
low, light
to light
between the buildings
like a snake when the rain is falling,
all over the city.

Mood music
After dinner
strokes her
soft up and
down then
it's pet time – play
the song FM
(that feels good)
there now
very soft out of the basket
coiling, sedately through the throb,
strings and a bold horn
savouring each note, (feels
good)
when the movement is over
a sly cough, shed the skin, sleeps
(good)

Hate
The snake in my hand
heart
instep
eats the blood, eats the whorl of my fingers
crunches the heel's tendon
soon it will shed me like a skin

Friend
Brothers now
the cuts on your hand, mine
joined, the blood
makes a snake's journey, less dry
than the wound of a stranger

Party
Someone has lost a snake.
She is standing at the party
holding it, bemused, not sure
whether the gentleman watching her
wishes to acknowledge ownership.
Put it in your bag, girl.

Ring
This snake has no beginning.
I make you a gift.
Wear it till the last wedding.

Growing
The snake takes off one skin
and does not return.
Sleep now. The air is passing, passing.

BEAST

Between nerve and
nerve, stretched
                    where desire
                                        jumps
the electric silences
between the cells
                    I keep
a certain hunger

muzzled. Its leash is tangled
under the skin. It walks through bone
as quietly as blood. It wears me
like old fur.

                    I take it on journeys
to and from
your face.

A COLONIAL AFFAIR

Let us practise, for want
of anything
to do today,
fellatio. For ease

I remove the skin, fore
and aft, you cover
the raw bulb with its warm one hundred
and forty-four square inches.
I am eager
(you do not care
for light, like bats
preferring the radar of shame
and the finger tease of touch)
now we become the same
colour, cats.

Among my souvenirs
there are stains
on your mouth that I may kiss
away. True, we make no children
at this violent union, but I have
bruised your tongue
with the hammer of history
and will you tell
what we did, what we did
in the dark? So I discharge
my debt, pretending mate

My black pawn takes your queen.
And dispossession coupling us
beyond release, this way
I come again
by the middle passage.

My bonds increase.

A DANDY DECEASED

She sucked him dry. Sex
was the reason he gave
for the green-bow bending of his will.
"Here, Here!" he commanded,
squirming in their lust,
and he clasped her
many-legged as a spider
must.
        Soon he was soft enough
to scoop up and swallow.
                        Now
the tough shell of his swagger swings
in her cocktail web, hollow.
While she preens
at parties he clings
to the skirts of her gossamer laughter,
little boy light.
                        Once spent,
all his time dancing
attendance. No more
the mating, no sex, no good, no
succour. He's happy this way back
into bachelorhood.

                        Don't sigh
it's a wonderful way for a dandy
to die. He's returned
to the comfort every grown lad needs –
fed her, and now he feeds.
                        He's come.
All the way home, to Mum.

VAMP

She rubbed her legs
together. The wives,
solicitously equal, bent away,
refusing to deride her
harsh complaint; contained
their itch to tell
the boastful bitch how
well their unflamboyant passion satisfied
and let her play the fool.

Smiled too, secure
to see their men
all eyes pretending interest
in poetic cool,
up-tight.
                    Outside, the cicada's long cry
shrilled sexlessly all night.

AFTER SUMMER, THE STRANGERS

After summer, the strangers
reappear, wearing their faces
like actors, changeable.
(How it go, how it go?)
Their names come to
the letter box haltingly.
I do not know
the language the air speaks
around them, their skins are
mapped with the scale dust
distances I have gone
without them.
                    If there are partings
this is one, this coming
like fish to a seasonal shore.

Impassively
the rooms acquire new
echoes, mirrors learn their eyes,
the path pretends their feet
are familiar, old
routes worn as that scuffed trunk,
these travel cases.
                         So many,
so many
summers

ECSTASIES: FOR MY DAUGHTER

If I could give you anything, it would be ecstasies:
times when a stranger's face opens to you so simply
you knew her always
days when the music in your head has shape and thunder
and all the dancers are in place
times when the grey world breaks like a diamond
and your hands are covered with glory, glory,
and every silence is a galaxy of faith

If I could give you anything
it would be fragments
of such beauty
all else would be forgiven

TESTAMENT: FOR A FRIEND'S CHILD

Because I hesitate,
seeing the way souls grow
in the brittle flesh
I do not sow
myself, but cultivate
poems instead,
preferring to attend
the gardens of my friend

And for you
without fear
accepting the world's fire
at the coming of age,
at the mind-smoke moods
when the heart learns
(growing to wood dark)
how the appetite burns,
I care.
I watch
how dry
new hurt arranges
your brambling hunger
into careful hedges
more becoming
a man; the casual
flesh coming to tinder
soon can
hold flame.
All ecstasy is fire,
what blesses, burns,
glory consumes the briar,
ash making.

So your green
leaf music breaking off,
I will you
tunes too glad
for time to still.
Now grow, heart
be not sad –
blaze and fulfil.
May crackling years
sing down their tongues
of flame, their fugues
of joy, their hymns:
a never ending fire
of alleluia in
your limbs

THREE

Because you bring me poems
I hold your hurting more
carefully
than this blind, bitter weather in my heart makes
just.

You are walking towards me
with all the parts of your self
sticking out
pure
poem

I said I'd throw no more
poems
but then you showed me
a mirror.
So now I am silent
to avoid
breaking

ALMS ON A TRAIN

but they all had to go, had to
go, there wasn't the time
to, the doors
spiracled once, sealed,
the slow earth made a noise
like rock shifting, the roof closed thunder
down over them, then

only the shudder and hurl through the dark
and eyes. Mirrors

staring at papers
covering themselves
watching the window
waiting to come to a place of silence

(earth falls in at the end,
always, the torn ground that never quite shuts)

and in his hand the note
sharp and white as a needle
song, stitched shadow against their mouth, unhealing
them

VERSION

Beg a ten cent mista –
de lickle bwoy sick, cyaan
eat (if him stop, who going to play
who going to play
who going to drop
who?)
All roun Jamdown
youtman a move –
one beat, yu no seet?
riddim sweet

but a soun cyaan full yu, yu
chuck an yu chuck
but de pocket have hole
an de lickle bwoy sick, sick
cyaan done. A neva see a rockers sweeta
dan rent when yu have it, a neva
catch a dubside dreada
dan bread if yu cyaan mek it –
da tune dey irie but a dead cyaan check it,
punch a nex one mista,
version!

…if de lickle bwoy dead, session done, bruck up
speaker an all, no-use
time (who going to dread
who going to dread
who going to bleed
who?) no more excuse-time; headline-news time,
running in de street time,
cool an red. Sky

juice time

WHASSIMATTER – YOU DON' KNOW ME NAME?

Don't call me brother, mother-!
I care
too. If you burn, I turn
black. If you're hung
up, Christ! man, I want to swing
with you. But
                    get this clear:
I'm pitching
on your side
because you're where the love is
at, and a maybe
chance for a legal dream or some
good thing. It's not
I like you, pal,
don't get me wrong, don't
want to eat or laugh or sleep with
you, and though
I'll bleed to bless you
(when I think
you're right) it's not
I'm always with you, just
with you against the mess you
fight. I fight it too.
But look, don't call me
brother. Use my name. And,
maybe,
I'll call
you.

FREEFALL

There are spaces
through which one may fall
without touching
the sides of shoulders or even
the edges of my own blood
where columns of laughter
bend their echoes
like toothpaste from a tube
between the plastic, brittle ends
of my haired nerves.
I have inherited
these empty plummetings
along with my electric toaster
and my stack-a-by chair
and the coded sounds I make
with my mouth
and the shape of my hand,
and a world that erodes
like a grain of sand.

My father has laboured long
with few tax exemptions
and a generous loving
to bring me these glitter-rare gifts
of his faith
and a broken and a contrite heart
shall I not despise.

And when I have made it
I shall pass on
all these and more
to my sons, for I love them
too
and the falling sickness.

LETTERS TO MY SON: V

I saw him this evening
watching the sky
fall, his face clean
clean like before
him Ma turn him out a de yard
fe locksing
half closing his eyes
the soft wet street
a cold hand on his skin

last time I see him
him sey   ah need clothes sah
maybe you can help me   I'm aksing you, please

couldn't look, I said yes
I can make it, I think,
I can make that next Friday, OK?
I'll be here, come in, OK?
and bought my way home
through the rain.
But he never came back.

And tonight I remember, the rain
falling sweet on the iron-blue leaves
by my window, I'm wishing
to dry his face,
dry his feet,
wrap him in something
thicker than memory

cover your face boy
the sky is falling
the houses are open
our children are standing
in rain

LETTERS TO MY SON: VIII

I am trying to live with the ease of those men,
foot-firm on the shelved sand.
They knit thick hands in the net. They fish silently.
The sea falls back through its weave
heavy as sleep,
or they couldn't work that weight, that green
muscle, could not bend
the clear-eyed fish from its furl, into air.

So I leave spaces in my life,
like the hungry silences of fishermen.
I tie words into rough threads
and drag with them
not what falls through, what leaves salt on the face,
but those quick, lovely images
that mind catches, leaping
among the day's drift
the heart's hurl
the blood's breaking
the web-twist of
this world's wet dazzle

LETTERS TO MY SON: IX

Watching your face
at the cat's lizard play
I understand you
becoming big enough to enjoy killing.
Do you know you are
making a sound with your throat,
a small movement in your feet?
Against that particular pleasure
I have, I confess,
no argument.

But later if you remember
the figures of this time –
hugging me hello after
the day's career into your open face,
the laughing
Sundays when your mother's whisper
has threaded us from dream, beginning us
into the honey silence of this house –

perhaps you will choose other music to dance to,
some colour than red
to wear in your hand
some taste than the dead
on your mouth

LETTERS TO MY SON: XI

Occasionally
when friends die
or an old photograph coughs from the crack of a drawer,
something walks, light
as an eyelash, falls
in a fine line to your face,
sits on your mouth, cold
as a dentist's drill
so that the name you speak is salt, and muffled.
He is lord of transience.
He is captain of loss.
He spits on your feed.
He eats it small.

But he doesn't understand loving, my son,
nor laughter. That is his lack.
Nor how you can keep them forever
by letting them leave.

So walk towards that hunger
pleasure haunted, come to all
this bright world
with your hand open, holding nothing
back.
Let him eat what you wanted.
Let him eat what you wanted.

POEM: FOR RAY

Your quiet hands
teach me confession

I absolve you
I absolve you
I absolve you

in the names of sunlight and silence and the secret
movements of the cell

go like any small creature, satisfied
with simple things:
to run   jump   fall   sleep through
wind
like

.Your hands are covered with birds
they fly for us

they fly for us
always

and now

SUNDAY GAME

he got up
he hit me
it hurt
he said quiet he said
go and play somewhere else
heres a pencil then go on draw
something but quietly

so now im making this picture to stop him
from being so angry
with sticks
for his hands and to walk on
that knob on top is his head
see his eyes are wide open
but now im filling them in and
when you turn it round it looks like hes
sleeping sssh

im putting lots of flowers all round him and
thats rain to make them grow
all slanty and sad and
lots of tall grass too
all round him
so quiet

I havent put him in a box yet
thats for right at the end

NIBBLESONG

Spring poems are over. My page
thickens with mousemarks. The paper
disintegrates: frost. A bulb dims
in the dusty sunlight, concealing
next year's green.

                    Sit on that bench. The men
chew heavy bread, argue endlessly,
low voices passing the chill evenings
mouth to mouth. Sometimes
a sheet slips from the table.
Catch it and read; it says
Call no man blessed
till. Where are the songs of.
What shall it profit a man. All
incomplete. Even the poems
that you sent her, nibbled

A COMMON PURSUIT

Fear wormed our eyes; the dark
inside our skulls
leaked hour-glass presentiments of dust;
voices uneven, soft.
                                        One lit a fire
telling some joke at the dead boy's expense.
We gathered round it
so it warmed our mouths, and flickered
and went out. And someone said
I didn't know him, but
he was a kind
of funny guy, imagining

him limp, so suddenly burnt
out; and his sculptor's hand dead-
heavy, like sand.
                                        So for a while
we talked instead of power
till the bright came back,
and tricks and women,
and things like that.

But the worms grow fat.

TWO

1.   Later, snow bandaged the room.
The clock was soft. It knew everything.
Your face healed into sleep.
Under my nails are scrapings from your life,
gathered while you laughed.

2.   Do you understand the Power?
I have given you my name.
I have eaten from your hand.
I have left skin on your pillow.
Now without pentacle or candles
you may summon me
at will. I am bound
to come.

A COMFORT OF CROWS

Mark this for a mercy: that here
birds, even here, sustain
the wide and impossible highways
of warm currents, divide the sky:
mark this – they all day have
amazed the air, that it falls apart
from their heavy wings in thin wedges
of sound; though the dull black earth
is very still, sweating
a special sourness
they make high over the hard thorn-trees
their own magnificence, turning,
they chain all together
with very slow journeys to and fro
the limits of the dead place,
smelling anything old and no longer quick.

Even here, though the rough ground
offers no kindness to the eye
nor the rusting engines could not ever
have intended an excellence of motion
and the stones have fallen in strange attitudes
and the boxes full of dry stained paper –
above the harsh barrows of land and metal
great birds pursue a vigilant silence.

The ceremonies of their soaring
have made a new and difficult solace:
there is no dead place nor dying so terrible
but weaves above it surely, breaking
the fragile air with beauty of its coming,
a comfort of crows.

POEM AGAINST GLORY

perhaps i ought to have said No
and died, heroes have
something of the holy about them
and mothers are used
to weep placidly
in the crossed attention of the arc lamps
achieving dignity before
the coffins' quiet
but the flesh persists
saying No to the flash
that burns everything
away
to the hurting that narrows
and tunnels finally
out
i will not
to the ecstasy that cuts bone breaks off light
like stalks of cane
so i played, Judas
and i write, poem
without music, but
strict, forgiving myself
as i forgive all those
who trespass against
dying. stubborn.

ICON

When, overhead, the slate
and thin shelled sky burns
dull red, leaping to white, breaks
like a child's face,
the stone stems of trees become opal,
rough and rust, the moon dim and recessional,

they are there, dew-maned;
I wake to the pure almond
of their eyes that gleam at me;

the grasshoppers, frightened, go to sleep,
the horses dragging me
through the sudden fields of sunlight.

I feed them
my grown heart –
by night it is whole again;
hooves shed with my flaked bone,
from my arms
the braided sinews
as thick as bird-cries
lift their throats
this way or that, reins.
They rest when I sleep
among the flat journeys of silence

but at dawn
they have not moved;
the comforting insects descend
on shy wings to a safe place, and
whinnying softly their shadows
approach the pale dreams
of my breath, they are waiting,
they accuse me,
neighing of death.

CORTÈGE

Their grief's wind blows him
three and a half miles home
to freedom, their black hands
limp, lowered like flags
feet stuttering
an alphabet of faith,

for his armour is
finally bronze, his weapon
silence and that green farm wagon
thousands attend, his chariot.

                    This last
march is the loneliest.
                    Yet
concealed, in the slow mules'
clatter, the mourners' feet
measuring loss
by the long Atlanta street

he shares a dream
that hope
in this funeral harvest of lilies will
let freedom ring,
the wounding, sworded South
healed in some ploughshare Spring.

COLLECTOR'S ITEM

It's out of place on the calm wall
of my middle-aging life, that print.
I had withdrawn my hate
from circulation.
But the curator scrabbles up
into my hand, hooks a long nerve into
the spine so it sees what I see
is me / not me, uses me. Thinks.
Its feet scratch
an old face out, slewed on the tilting poem, thickens a line,
breaks
one, compares the memory, recovers
a perfect image.
The animal jacks deeper
into pain.
Like a child screaming
I shake it from my back,
disconnecting.

I.C.U.

Sometimes I drive too fast, not noticing
the accidents of flesh.
Fly flag, show red, call. Or
I will not see
the ripped skin, the bones breaking.
Cold in my ambulance
I'll wait your signal
in the scrubbed room of my want
to help, playing patience,
and when the funerals pass
lifting dust drowsily
against the evening windows
I'll watch the mourners curiously
wondering that
no-one had said: Slow down, stop,
we are hurt, we are
all of us
dying.

GAME

Simon says feel
Simon says cry
Simon says sing
Simon says think
Simon says laugh
Die

POEM AGAINST MAGIC: FOR MELLA

They say that before the bullet
enchanted him in his shirt
which changed wonderfully
to the colour of the flag, Mella
whispered
the name of the President,
that's how they knew,
that's how they knew.

Well, I'll drum you a poem underground
(his tricks have no power over that sound)
I'll sing you a song under my breath:
the name of the President is Death.

Come then. There is not
much time. No longer.
Here is my shirt. Don't wait for a shot
to magic it red. Share what is yours
and grow stronger
and grow stronger

than that Person:
mas fuerte
que el Presidente
Muerte.

DIARY OF A COUNTER-REVOLUTIONARY

He doesn't sleep.
I smell him in the mornings
thin and grey, he wears the stale smoke
of Apocalypse. Stands all day, out
of work. Maybe just shifting. Barely
breaking the wind.

I hurry breakfast,
finding the office keys. Long before eight.
And he's there.
Whittling
my world down silently. Stands,
ceremonial like a knife, sheathed

in his isolation. Sometimes I
sign letters: but across the window he
practises throwing his shadow so
its dull blade-fall
skewers my door
and clatters on the wall.
Doesn't talk though, never knocks,
wouldn't answer. Smiles. But I'm sure

I know what he wants
me to do. I've thought about
letting my hair grow down
and my nails, and smoke
like a halo around
the golden, massive Word
that Jah spoke. Well, it's not fair
to expect
me
to give up
kindnessmodernjazzmetrecalforlunchand

my warm little house
with its own little garden gate for
some paradise of his
righteous hate.

And I'm scared to
death. He's watching me,
cold every night. And shivering

in his scabbard.

TIE

A wi tell yu: a cyaan leave. A cyaan
cut, a captcha, dis place
hole I, cyaan go – hear
mi now. Drum. Di feet
drummin. But a
doan know. A doan know
anadda way to walk,
a cyaan talk
sep di word come
soundin so. A cyaan show
nuttn dat sharpa dan salt
in di eye like sea
dat hot in di bone like
dis sun.
        Long clime, long time – fi wi
sorrow like seed
fall, cry. Slow. Haulin di hillside
fi hunga. But I grow
here, slave
in dis green still. Cyaan get aweh,
cyaan get aweh, cyaan
twine out.

TRAVELLING LIGHT

I packed again today. Not much.
A letter never answered, asking
for love, or money. Questions.
In the right light
they explode to trees.
I mark them on the map.
A few people, dug in
behind one corner of my grin – guerrillas
against the bitter times.
They lick the blood off
when cold cracks my bone.
A small bird, bearing
news from the front.

ON THE EDGE

eyes remain open, dry
light fires them to porcelain
the cracks turn into roots
trees
cathedrals
finally

coffins
on the edge

you learn
to practise living
without excuses
without shadow

sharpening your life
every day
draws a hot clear line across
the skin, fat falls off

there is a certain satisfaction from
questions articulated
like bone under the appetites

SUMMERSONG

These are the months of bloom and wind and blight,
silence and fire. Storm is in the air.
Time now to watch against the long days' light.

Mine is a summer clock: it tells the year
is half past living, and the minutes wind
away from spring to darkness. Frost is near.

But through your flesh drums something undefined,
a pulsing that denies the season's flight,
a celebration beating in the mind.

So keep you tranquil at the summer's height,
shadow this house until the fields are bare
and autumn leaves, and leaves you burning bright.

REPORT

on some hunting customs in the Greater Antilles

One. Colours of the hunt:
They mark the houses
with silence, and dark-
en the rooms. To begin,
some lone cub's howling
drifts like a river
between villages. The tangled green
cages of history are open, and echo.
This is a country used
to dispossessions – each year they re-enact
some ritual death. Remorseless, exact.
One morning   when the wind
shivers and wipes the sun's eye clean
in the sky
there are whispers
of whiteness.

Two. The psychology of the hunt: It is
a tribal affair.
They ask
        who is this
        sitting among the warriors,
        breathing our air?
        Beware the cunning of age
        and compassion in this face,
        how does he dare
        to advise us?
Those without teeth
are driven away from the fires,
the sleeping places
are swept clean, their names are taken.

Silence his voice
before his vision leads us
back to the cages we have forsaken.
There is blood on their faces.

Three. Recommendations:
Year after year
the old ones die. Nothing is surer.
The young bloods hunt
to show their strength
and the tribe is poorer.
And those who build the council house
today, tomorrow
may have to hide from the council. Perhaps
that is cause
for sorrow.

GOODBYESONG

Now at the moon's edge
shadows. Leave all, turning
from playground dances into quieter journeys.
We always knew the quick, splendid affections
of this carnival would fade
to different faces, tent and field exchanged
for the applause of other, darker places. So

no sadness. Give rooms back
to silence. Let the sea repeat
unwatched, its long, salt hymn.
That moon's brief white instructs us:
own each moment,
before the dances and the faces dim.

HEALSONG 1

Between the wave's mouth
and the stone's consent;

the painted moment
before resolution
after the question
when it is as if
the spray will never happen.

Enter that silence.
The visions will dry on your eyes
like salt, the world will become
opaque.
The heart
will place like a hand on
the sky's clock
wedges between
the devouring pain and the bone's surrender.
Be patient.
Like stone.

SCENE

Rose on the table.
This grey ward, joyful, takes fire.
The sun falls west. Ash.

Rain slants to the street.
Nurses talk outside my room,
voices like soft earth

The surprise of wild flowers!
Walls fall open, roofs melt.
I too grow sunwards.

BUTTERFLY DREAM

You saw me dancing? Wasn't ecstasy.
Was shaking loose the gut and the bones
and the flesh, I was trying to take off
wanted to fly easy as air off
the sad ground.
                    Watch me grin. I practise constantly.
They say it's a long time after
earth sucks the soft parts away, before
there's only dust; I want to look my best
during that silence. Tranquil. Teeth.

And see me hold my love: see terror.
We pretend there's someone there, we two
invent each other, we two name the stranger
two skins away, falling together.

Watch me sleep. I'm listening to the traffic
of my dreams. At every intersection of the cells
the light goes green. I hear my life roar home
(memory rattles. Thunder!) Peak hour.
I'm alive. At last.

SHADOWSONG

Waiting, I watch the shadow on that wall.
It says that surely, though I cannot see
the sun is burning on its long, slow fall
into the night that brings you in to me.

The curtains move as silently as you
once drew them close to make a loving place.
Evening will come. Nothing the world may do
can stop the shadows turning to your face.

THE EDITOR

He's coming, that One
who will justify all
at the margin
black all of a sudden
sound, light, mass
fall into his hand. The event-
horizon collapses, the picture winks
in and keeps going. He'll touch, in
no hurry at all
when the evening
cools, slips on a skin
someone threw away
smooths it down over his face
is a friend perhaps

since there's no point
these at least I salvage:
a poem, my laughter

in spite of that blue hand that
could be here, now,
shaping the end of my line
to his

ABOUT THE AUTHOR

DENNIS SCOTT (1939-1991) earned a first-class degree in English from the University of the West Indies and a Drama in Education diploma from the University of Newcastle-upon-Tyne. From 1977 until 1983 he was Director of the Jamaica School of Drama. In 1983 he was a Visiting Professor in Directing at the Yale School of Drama, and he remained there to become Acting Chairman, Playwrighting, in 1984 and Co-Chairman, Directing, in 1986. He was a director at the National Playwrights' Conference at the Eugene O'Neill Theatre Centre and a consultant to the Playwrights-in-Residence Program at the Julliard Theatre Centre. His own plays include *The Crime of Anabel Campbell*, *An Echo in the Bone*, *Dog* and *Live and Direct from Babylon*. His books of poetry are *Uncle Time*, *Dreadwalk*, *Strategies* and the present collection. He received many awards, including (from the Institute of Jamaica) a Silver Musgrave Medal for achievement in poetry.